MUM'S
GUIDE
TO THE
UNIVERSITY
SEARCH

MUM'S GUIDE TO THE UNIVERSITY SEARCH

Dagmar Morris

The Book Guild Ltd

First published in Great Britain in 2017 by
The Book Guild Ltd
9 Priory Business Park
Wistow Road, Kibworth
Leicestershire, LE8 0RX
Freephone: 0800 999 2982
www.bookguild.co.uk
Email: info@bookguild.co.uk
Twitter: @bookguild

Copyright © 2017 Dagmar Morris

The right of Dagmar Morris to be identified as the author of this
work has been asserted by her in accordance with the
Copyright, Design and Patents Act 1988.

All rights reserved. No part of this publication may be
reproduced, transmitted, or stored in a retrieval system, in any form or by any means,
without permission in writing from the publisher, nor be otherwise circulated in
any form of binding or cover other than that in which it is published and without
a similar condition being imposed on the subsequent purchaser.

Typeset in Minion Pro

Printed and bound in the UK by TJ International, Padstow, Cornwall

ISBN 978 1911320 562

British Library Cataloguing in Publication Data.
A catalogue record for this book is available from the British Library.

Contents

Acknowledgements

Mum's Guide to the University Search would not have been written without the support of my family, who have been a big source of encouragement. Firstly, I'd like to thank my husband Tony who has always been there and said that "I should just do it", so I have. Secondly I would like to thank my daughter Ellen who spent a lot of time proofreading the book for me whilst really not having the time to do so, as she was studying for her degree in English literature and Creative Writing. Thirdly my thanks go to my other daughter Chloe, who has allowed me the time and space to make this happen.

My love to all of you and my thanks for all your encouragement, championship, backing and blessing.

Many sources have been used in the research for this book, most notably from GOV.UK, MoneySavingExpert. com, MSE News, Oxbridge, The Russell Group, *The Telegraph* Student Life Section, UCAS and UEA.

Foreword

Dagmar Morris lives in Essex with her husband and two daughters. The eldest is twenty-two and has recently left university; she was the inspiration for the book.

Dagmar has had an interesting and varied career and has vast experience with dealing with the general public and relating to how they think and what their expectations are. She has worked for several fashion companies in marketing and public relations and has gone onto work for financial institutions in London, dealing with banking and broker sectors. She started her own freelance beauty business when her children arrived, whilst being a Director and Company Secretary for her husband's consultancy firm. She has since moved on to work for the Fire Service in Essex, dealing with community liaison. However, foremost she is a Mum.

The book explains in detail the university process from a parent's perspective. When her eldest daughter was at the stage of looking into universities she realised the complexity of it and found there was nowhere she could turn for help. It was at this point that Dagmar began to write the guide about the journey of the university search, to help other parents prepare for the oncoming experience and events. It covers from the beginning of qualifying the university to her daughter being settled into a job.

**

A clue is most definitely in the title! If you are like I was and are clueless about the university pilgrimage, or if you just need some tips as to where to start the journey looking into universities for your charge or charges, then this book was written for you.

DM xx

www.facebook.com/mumsguidetotheuniversitysearch

Introduction

Mum's Guide to the University Search... A year in your life that you will never get back!

... So why did I write the guide? I want to warn, give tips (the first of these tips being to drink wine), advise, to try to make the university search experience as painless as possible. Let me know if I succeed.

It really does take a year – a whole year. A friend of mine organised a fund raiser belly dancing night which I missed due to seeing 12 universities in about 6-8 weeks. We had to have our university forms in early to catch the Oxbridge applications. Theirs has to be in by October time. The form for all the other universities is due in January, which is much more civilised as you have more time to prepare.

Things that I would suggest you do look into, find out about and think seriously about before starting are...

1

Qualifying the university

Helping your charges decide how to qualify universities is the first task that needs to be tackled. This is a big step as it is the foundations of the whole process. Some of the steps that I would advise you to get your children to focus on are as follows:

What do they want to study at uni? Make sure they have the required subjects to do the degree. Make sure it is something they are passionate about, otherwise they could be wasting three years of their lives and a huge amount of money.

Get them to find out what the syllabus is for the subject they want to study, and decide if this is what they had in mind and are interested in. My daughter went to study English Literature with Creative Writing, which is fantastic. However, English can be studied at most universities, so she needed to make sure that the syllabus appealed to her and was what she actually wanted to study. They shouldn't just wing this. There is no point going to a university thinking that a course will entail what they want to study when actually they end up doing

1

the part of the subject that they least enjoyed at sixth form/college. Courses may vary from uni to uni, so don't expect that the modules will all be the same.

They will need to find out what their predicted grades are. They will be able to ask their teachers for this information. Then they need to find out what grades the chosen university requires for them to do the course they want to study. They have to make sure this matches up to their predicted grades, or grades that their teachers realistically think is possible for them to achieve. It's great to aim high, but if they don't get the correct grades they'll have to go through something called Clearing, which is added stress.

It is a good idea to check out the top 100 UK universities providing the subject they wish to study. Go to the web and look up the top 100 universities. I found some sites that were interesting and useful:

www.thecompleteuniversityguide.co.uk/league-tables/rankings

www.timeshighereducation.co.uk/world-university

Look into the league tables on National Student Survey (NSS) and look up the subject rating. Also check out http://unistats.com/. There is also information from the newspapers such as the *Telegraph* and the *Guardian*. Again, this can be looked up on the internet.

Is your child aiming for a Russell Group university? What is The Russell Group, I hear you ask? Well, it was established in 1994. It was set up to represent its member's views on the current position and the future of higher education through discussions with the government, funding bodies, and other higher education groups. It made its views known through its research publications and in the media. It is a group of twenty-four British public research universities. Russell Group members received approximately two-thirds of all university research grant and contract income in the United Kingdom in 2010. They are compared with the Ivy League, the high-ranking private universities in the United States. So if your child is aiming high this is a good group to look into.

Do they want to go away from home to university, or would they prefer to stay closer to home? There are obviously advantages and disadvantages for both of these. Staying closer to home is cheaper as they may not need the maintenance loan, which is a loan to rent accommodation whilst at university. This loan does result in extra debt for your child later on and if they are a home bird, going to a university which is closer to you may be the right option. However, a lot of students want to go away to get the full 'university experience' and feel they become a much more independent person because of this. Everyone is different. They need to pick the option that is right for them. They definitely *shouldn't* just do what their friends are doing.

Disqualify areas you don't want them to travel to. Make this decision before they are too far down the qualification process. For instance, they might feel happier if the journey home is not too far or difficult. On the other hand being a long way from home may give them more of an independent experience. Go to look at the area to see if it's right for them, if the place feels right, if it feels safe. What looks great in a brochure might not be such a great location in real life. Obviously what they want to study may have a bearing on this. If they want to study something like English, most universities do offer this so you have a huge choice. If they want to study something more niche they may be restricted by where the subject is actually run. Both scenarios have positives and negatives. If the subject they want to study is popular they will have a huge choice of where to go and look, but there will be more competition and pressure to achieve higher grades. If their subject is more niche they may be restricted by where they can go and look, but the process of finding and viewing the universities will be more straightforward.

They should speak to their school/college to get advice. The teachers all have degrees. Most have been to university and should be able to give them some guidance; however, not all schools are particularly effective in doing this so you may need to speak to friends and family who have had experience of the university search.

Go to any meetings set up through the school/college by university personnel. Even if they have no interest in going to that university it is a really good idea to attend these, as these meetings can give you all lots of information which the school/college may not know. And they can make you feel a bit more relaxed about the sort of tutors that the universities have and the way they run.

2

Attending a school meeting about university

My daughter's school held a meeting for parents whose children were considering going to university. The idea was for them to talk us through the basics and to answer questions. This was extremely helpful, and if your school does this I would highly recommend that you attend. They also invited a lecturer to speak about their university, and again answer any questions. This was an extremely useful meeting and really was the start of the whole process from our point of view as parents.

Make sure that if you have any questions you are ready to ask them. When our daughter went to university she was in the first year of the new loan scheme. Lots of the questions that year were from parents concerned about that. Some of the questions I wanted to ask were as follows:

- *What is the difference between the loans?*
  One loan is for the university education, and goes straight to the university. This is called the tuition loan. The second loan is for living costs and accommodation. This is called the maintenance loan.

- *What help are families entitled to have in order to pay for university?*
  There is special help for families on low income, but *all* families are entitled to a tuition fee loan. How much maintenance loan is offered to you will depend on your personal household income circumstances.

- *Where can you apply for the student loans?*
  Student finance England. This is explained in more detail when you are actually looking around universities. You can also go to https://www.gov.uk/student-finance/overview, which will give you further information.

- *How does the tuition loan work?*
  This is paid directly to the university. The earliest you'll start repaying the loan is the April after you leave the course. This will only come into effect once your annual income is over £21,000 per year. If your income drops below this amount you stop paying.

- *How does the maintenance loan work?*
  This is paid directly to the student in three instalments at the beginning of each term. It is important that a student bank account is set up for this purpose. The maintenance loan is the loan where different amounts are offered depending on personal or family circumstances.

- *The student costs went up to 6-9K in 2012, depending on the university. Can you pay the 6-9K off yearly over the three years at university?*
  The answer is yes.

- *Can you pay part of the 6-9K off yearly?*
  Again the answer is yes, but this is not advised. It is better to either pay off all the costs in full or go down the student loan route. To mix and match doesn't give much benefit as the final payments of the student will not be apparent until they graduate and these will fluctuate depending on their financial situation throughout their lives. So you as a parent may be paying over the top by part-paying their university costs. However, this is a personal decision and one that you must feel comfortable with.

- *After they have finished university, can they pay off their debt early? For example, if they are earning good money, can they clear their debt early or at least pay amounts off upfront?*
  There are no penalties for paying some or the entire loan off early. www.studentloanrepayment.co.uk

- *What other costs should we consider?*
  Accommodation is the main extra cost, but travel and food are others to include. There are also costs that you may not have even thought about, such as a bus pass to get them around their university town.

- *How can these be managed financially?*
  The answer we were given was the student loans. But if you are not eligible for extra financial help on top of the maintenance loan, as far as travel and food are concerned this is Bank of Mum & Dad's responsibility. However, if you are on a low income, there is more assistance given.

- *How many universities should we look at?*
  The answer was lots, as many as you can make time for.

- *When do the Open Day events start?*
  These differ from university to university. You can find this information out on the university websites, but they usually start in June/July in their AS year or September/December in their A Level year, prior to application. You may need to book onto Open Day events so pay attention as to when booking onto these events starts. This can be four weeks prior to the event or even earlier.

- I asked about the structure of the percentage of interest that they will pay on their loans. This can be looked into at the finance meeting/lecture at the universities on the open day, or there are some good websites that explain this.

- *What is the difference between scholarships/bursaries/ grants and fee waivers?*
  Scholarships/bursaries are for students who are

exceptionally bright. They are an incentive for that student to go to that university. Grants are given as extra help to low-income families. You do not have to be of a certain academic standard to receive a grant. As long as you are accepted into the university, if you have a low income, you can receive a grant. Fee waivers are a reduced tuition price that can be offered to students from low-income families.

3

Application process

Things which need to be done for the application process are as follows:

A personal statement is required by the universities as part of their application. Your school/college should help you with this. Ask them to give input as to what is needed to maximise the impact of your statement.

A reference is required from the sixth form/college that your child has attended for the university application. The school/college will provide this, but make sure this is in progress at the appropriate time. The reference should be written by a Head of Year or Head of Sixth Form.

You will need to register with The Universities and Colleges Admissions Service, otherwise known as UCAS, in the autumn. UCAS opens for applicants in September of the year of application. This is a pain in the backside as you feel like you are paying money for nothing at the start of the process, as far as a parent is concerned anyway. However this is the body to help with the administration with university applications. There is a charge for this, but just pay it. It is not an exorbitant amount, but believe me, the further down the road you get with the university experience, UCAS is the least of your worries. Actually, when they get their results through you realise that UCAS is worth their salt as they do take the pressure off at this point – A BIT. Firstly, if they have their first choice or second choice it is from UCAS that they find this information out from. If they don't and they have to go through Clearing UCAS are instrumental in this process and are invaluable.

Your child should apply to the universities of their choice. Depending on what course you apply for and where you want to go your application should be with UCAS by these dates in the calendar year. Check with the school what the actual dates are for the year you are applying in.

- Apply during mid *October* for the universities of Oxford, Cambridge or any professional course in medicine, veterinary medicine, science and dentistry.
- Apply during mid *January* for the majority of courses.
- Apply during mid/end *March* for some art and design courses
- The end of *June* is the absolute last date to apply for the majority of courses. However, this is not recommended, as you may not get onto the course of your choice.

REMEMBER: applications need to be in by October if applying to Oxbridge. Make sure you really want to go to these universities if you apply to them, as it can add extra stress if it is not highly desired.

When applying to Oxbridge they may ask for the student to do a pre-requisition application exam relevant to what they are studying. Oxbridge will let your school know that your child is applying to them and the school should then assist with letting your child take the exam at school. Make sure this is done at the appropriate time.

Any university that they are applying to may also ask for pre-application submissions. They may require a sample of their work to qualify them for the course that they wish to study. For instance, my daughter was asked for an essay to be sent to Oxford and a piece of creative writing to be sent to the University of East Anglia to qualify her for the degree that she wanted to study. Make sure that these pieces of work are sent by the required deadlines.

After the application has been sent, they may be required to attend an interview. This interview may help the university to decide which grades they would like the student to attain. If they really like the candidate, they may even give an unconditional offer. This means they can attend that university, no matter what they achieve.

Useful web addresses are:

www.ucas.com
www.ucas.com/apply

Once they have applied to the universities of their choice they can stay in contact with the university via the admissions office. It is the admissions office who they should contact if they have any questions. The admissions office are also who they should keep in touch with to keep them up to date with their academic situation if your child has any concerns; for example, if they want to check that the pre-application submissions have reached the university, if they are worried that they may not get the required grades, if they want to change the course or even if you have family issues or an illness which may affect their grades. It is important to have the admissions office telephone number to hand once they have made their choices of universities, whatever their situation.

Dates of procedures – Note that this process starts from one year before the final year of sixth form/college – do not wait until final year of A level study, as you may miss out on open days.

February onwards:
- Look into when the tours are on at the universities you want to go and look at and register for undergraduate open days.
- Note: they are all at different times of the year.

April-December onwards:
- Open day tours and events.

September
- UCAS opens for applicants.
- Apply for student finance through Student Finance England online.
- Apply shortly after completing UCAS form.

Nov-March:
- Receive replies from universities with offers and interview requests.

April-May
- Choose firm and insurance choices; the 5 choices have to be cut down to 2.

August
- Receive results.
- Possible adjustment period to change the course or utilise Clearing.
- Accept university place.
- Accept accommodation place.

4

Money

This next bit is going to sound very practical and boring, but stay with me because it is important.

This seems obvious, but I will point it out to you because someone who has no experience of university loans/grants may find it confusing. The tuition loan is to cover the costs of the tuition. The maintenance loan/grant is to cover the cost of living (basically, the rent). Families on lower incomes may receive maintenance grants. From the 2016/17 academic year, government changes may mean that maintenance grants are scrapped. It is proposed that all the money for maintenance will now come as a student loan. Maximum borrowing will be increased for the new students from 2016. In the past the tuition loans went straight to the university. The maintenance loan came in three instalments a year as each semester began. There had to be some flexibility with regards to this as sometimes the money was delivered after the rent money for their accommodation was required. Be aware of that so they don't go in the red due to any delay in receiving their loan. To stop this from becoming a problem, you might want to think about being flexible in allowing your child some cash flow.

The school should give them the application form for the loans in their final year. This has to be sent off to the Local Education Authority (LEA), who assess parental income. Student loans come from the Student Loans Company, which is a government department. They should send all the necessary forms a few months in advance of starting university, but keep an eye on this. The LEA and/or the Student Loans Company are the two main providers. See www.gov.uk/browse/education and www.gov.uk/student-finance. Be aware the loans can be applied for before having a confirmed place at university.

The loans are means-tested, which means the loan offered depends on your household income, with 65% of the loan guaranteed and 35% income assessed. Everyone eligible will be entitled to a loan regardless of parental income. Household income of £25,000 or below will be applicable to get the maximum loan offer.

The student will pay one repayment amount per month, but only after graduation. Repayments will be based on whatever the % rate of that time was agreed after they are earning £21,000.00 and over for a maximum of thirty years. At this present time that % is 9% of everything they earn over £21,000.00. This is proportional to the salary that they earn. Repayments will be collected via the tax systems and will come straight out of their pay packet. The loan will be written off after thirty year's post-graduation.[1]

---

1   At the time of writing all figures were correct. However these may now have changed. No liability will be accepted.

During university:

- Cumulates RPI inflation coupled with 3% on the outstanding balance. This is until the first April after graduation.

Post university:

- Income under £21,000 – Cumulates RPI inflation
- Income £21,000.00-£41,000.00 – Interest will be RPI to RPI + 3% income dependent. These figures are fixed until 2021, but may change thereafter.
- Income £41,000.00 plus – Cumulates RPI inflation + 3%

This may change every year depending on inflation.

To find out what your payments might be go to https://www.gov.uk/student-finance/overview and use the repayment calculator.

The loan system can be quite confusing, but information should be available at the school university meeting, if they do one. You can also find out more information at the universities when you go to them. They usually provide a finance meeting on their visit days.

There are also websites that you can look at to get more information about student finance. Here are some useful ones:

www.gov.uk/student-finance
www.studentloanrepayment.co.uk
www.moneysavingexpert.com

Most universities will also have their own web section about finance on their sites.

Also, make sure you look into any assistance that you may be applicable for, such as Scholarships, Student Loans and Bursaries.

Scholarships may be offered for academic excellence. If, for example, your child obtains three or four A*s the university may offer a monetary scholarship package. This will vary depending on the university, so be careful to check which grades will give you a scholarship at each individual university.

Student Loan for maintenance is to help with living costs. The amount students receive will depend on their family's household income. 65% of the loan being guaranteed and 35% income assessed. This means everyone eligible is entitled to a loan, regardless of how much their parents earn. Households earning £25,000 or under will be eligible for the maximum amount of assistance.

If the household income is under a certain limit you may also be eligible for Income Support or certain other means-tested benefits such as Housing Benefit, you may be able to get other assistance to help with additional course related costs such as books, equipment, travel or childcare.

You may be eligible for assistance if you:

- are a single parent;
- have a partner who is also a student and one or both of you is responsible for a child or young person under twenty who is in full-time education;
- have a disability;

- qualify for Disabled Students' Allowances;
- have been unable to work for a continuous period of time, at least twenty-eight weeks;
- are waiting to go back to a course after an agreed time out due to an illness or caring responsibility that has now ended;

Examples of the evidence you may send include:

- a birth certificate or passport;
- a letter from your college or university;
- a copy of your tax credit award;
- a letter from the Department for Work and Pensions to show you receive single parent benefit;
- a letter, on headed paper, from a professional authority that can assure you are a single parent. This can be from a doctor, lawyer, teacher, police officer or minister of religion for example.

Make sure you complete your online application to ensure you receive your full entitlement to Student Finance.

Bursaries are extra financial help from universities and colleges for students from low-income families. Bursaries do not have to be paid back usually.

To receive a bursary you have to apply directly to the organisation that gives them out, i.e. the university or college that you are applying to. They will be able to tell you if you qualify.

If you receive a Student Loan for maintenance you may still get a bursary, depending on the university or college you attend.

The amount you are entitled to receive can be different depending on the university or college you go to, so you should contact them directly to find out more about the bursaries they offer.

Each university or college has their own rules about bursaries, scholarships and awards. For example:

- who qualifies
- how much you can get
- how to apply

Talk to the student support service to find out what's available.

The bursary can be one or more of the following:

- a cash bursary up to a certain amount
- help with tuition fees and accommodation
- a free foundation year (a programme that helps students meet the entry criteria for a higher education course)

If you're awarded a cash bursary it's paid directly into your bank account by your university or college. Contact your university or college to find out how and when to apply.[2]

The money side of it is SCARY, definitely. I was someone brought up thinking that debt was bad, and I found this part of the university experience exceptionally difficult. As a parent you feel that you should be able to

---

2   At the time of writing all figures were correct. However these may now have changed. No liability will be accepted.

support your daughter/son in paying for university, or at least go some way towards it. Unfortunately, the figures are so big now that unless you can pay it off completely, a loan, for most people, has to be a part of the equation. The best thing, unless you are fortunate enough to be able to pay it all off up front, is to let the pupil going to university take all the student scholarships, loans, bursaries etc. that are on offer. It is them, after all, who is going to university, not us!

You will still be bank of Mum and Dad, even without the loan situation. The loans don't cover everything. If you are not on benefits their loans will not be as much as those who are and there is usually a deficit in what the loan covers for rent, let alone anything else. Your child still has to eat, remember, so there is food to be bought. Most courses will require books so there is a cost for all the books that need to be bought. Travel needs to be considered; how they are going to travel to and from uni may be expensive. Trips back home at Christmas, Easter, weekends for family occasions will need to be thought about and catered for. Travel when they are at uni should also be considered. Some universities have excellent bus links to the local town and may even offer a student bus pass deal, which can be beneficial to them whilst studying. Make sure they have an affordable and versatile mobile phone contract. This will be their phone and you don't want them to be worried about the cost of this, but you also don't want to pick up a large bill from them. Check their tariff and make sure it is what is required. Does it have enough minutes for them to call you on, enough texts and other special features for contact with you while they are away? All these extras have to be thought about. You will find that a fairly substantial amount of support is still needed. It's normal to want to give them too much money – many parents feel the need to give their children monthly allowances. But this does not help your child to be independent in the long-run. Encourage them to get student jobs. This is good experience for them in the world of work. It can also go onto their CV when they are looking for work at the end of their university life to show future employers that they have already experienced the work market whilst studying for their degree.

In conclusion, I found that the only way I could justify the loan situation was to think of it as a student tax rather than a student loan. If someone told you that you were expected to pay your adult child's taxes you would tell them to b****r off. You would feel that, as an adult, they could, and should, pay their own taxes, wouldn't you? There has to be some point when they are expected to act as the adults they have become. And anyway, as the government keeps telling us, they will be earning more than we ever did because they have gone to university. Let's see how true that is, shall we?

5

Trekking around the shortened List

So now it's time to get down to business. The preliminary exercises have been started. The next phase is the trekking around the shortened list, and visiting the universities that have some possibility of making the short list on your child's application form. So get your trainers out, and find a good rucksack for packed lunches, and pads and pens.

I think we saw fifteen in about six-eight weeks. This sounds like a lot, I know, and it was exhausting. I can't deny that; however, it was definitely a worthwhile exercise. At the time I might not have agreed with this statement, but looking back on it I am very pleased we did it.

You learn a lot about the universities, and believe me, they are not all the same. Some of them are very highbrow and others are more like colleges. Some of them are very large and some are smaller and more intimate. It really depends on what your child feels comfortable with, and to be honest, they won't really know what they feel comfortable with until they go and have a look. Also to note, when we went to visit there were certain universities that we went to look at because they had very good reputations. Just be aware that a good reputation doesn't necessarily mean that it's the type of university you are looking for. When we were there, we knew very quickly which universities were not the ones for us. This is why it is important to go and look, because whilst it may look very good on paper, when you actually get there and look around it may be totally wrong for you. This may not be for any particular reason other than you being uncomfortable with the feel of the university. So it is definitely worth going to look, and I would recommend the more the better.

So from about 100 top universities you shorten your list to as many as you can fit in to visit, until the application has to be sent off. As I said, we saw about fifteen universities. But we were doing the Oxbridge application, and if you aren't doing that you have more time, and could probably fit in more. All the universities have open days, but we found quite a few had open days on the same day, which was frustrating. This leads to prioritisation and diary management. However, if this happens you could also go to the universities under your own initiative, and do a self-tour. We did do some self-tours, and as with most things, there are advantages and disadvantages for both.

The open days are very informative, very busy and you get to see A LOT, but without a doubt they are showcases. Not that this is bad, we all love a good show and they can be very exciting and exhilarating for the person wishing to go. The self-tours are good because you get to see the university as it is, with students going about their daily business. This was very good as you get a real feel as to what the students are like. The down side of this was you didn't get to see everything, or meet any of the lecturers, which can make you feel a bit as though you're missing out. For example, you won't see any of the student accommodation on a self-tour. Also, if you do a self-tour be aware that even with a map, you will probably get lost. However when this happened to us, (which it did on several occasions), we found it was a great way to meet some of the students, who we found were all extremely helpful and very nice. This gave us extra confidence in the university we were looking at.

6

At the university

What are you looking for? When you are at the university you might not know what you are looking for or what you want from a university, but you will know what you don't like and you will know what feels right and comfortable. Obviously most of it will feel a bit strange to begin with because it is new and a different environment from school or college, but the more universities you go to look at, the more confident you will be with what feels right.

- Does your child want the university to be in faculties or not? This is where the different schools of study are set out in different buildings. The larger universities and the higher-ranking universities tend to have faculties. This just makes it easier for the university to deal with the separate subjects by giving them their own specific areas within the university. They might like the fact that the university is split into faculties; on the other hand, they might prefer the university to feel more intimate and for the subjects not to be split up so definitely. The smaller universities do not always have such a variety of subjects and therefore faculties are not required.

- Do they want a large campus university feel where there are shops, restaurants, a bank and everything on site, or a smaller university with shops and everything else off campus? Note that if smaller universities do not have facilities such as shops and restaurants on-site, this is usually because they are very close to, or in, a city that provides all of these things.

These questions can be answered at an open day. The open days are well worth attending, as there is a wealth of information on tap. Even if you can't get to all the open day events of the universities that you are considering, it is important that you attend as many as you can to get a real feel for the university and the students who attend it.

This is what you should expect from an open day:

- Look at the grounds of the university. Go on a tour. Get a feel for the surroundings. Learn how the university is set out and the facilities surrounding it. For instance, what shops are available on campus? Does it have a super-market/food shop, a café, a bank, a bookshop? What is the on-site library like? Does it have fitness facilities? Some even have swimming pools. Which of these, if any, are important for what your child wants to gain from the university experience?
- Go to the welcome meeting. This is where the basics of the university are explained. How it is

set up, what is on the university campus, what is expected of students and parents and when it is expected to be handed into the university. They will also talk about accommodation information, restaurant information or the food situation. Some universities will have food plans which parents can sign up to so that they know their children will be fed at least in the first year! Other universities have completely self-catered accommodation.

- Go to a lecture of the subject that your child wants to study at university and talk to the lecturers. By talking to the lecturers they will get a very good feel about the course and if it is right for them. Also ask how many contact/teaching hours they will have in a week. This might shock you as it may not be as many as you are expecting, but this can be because of the way the course is set up; for instance, there may be a lot of reading required for the course, and therefore there may be significantly less contact hours.

- The accommodation meeting will explain all you need to know about where your child is going to live for their first year of university. Most universities try to offer first year students residence of some sort. Note that in some universities, such as Oxbridge, accommodation is provided for the entire course of being a student. After the first year, students are usually provided with guidance for future accommodation. The meeting will explain when you need to apply for on-site accommodation, which is usually by the end of June in the year prior to entry of uni. You will find out how long the licence agreement will be: usually thirty-eight weeks starting September to June, but this can vary depending on the university. It will explain who has the priority of receiving university accommodation, depending on how far away you live from the university. You should explore what type of accommodation is on offer, as usually there are quite a few different options to choose from. It will explain what else may be included. Some universities include utility rooms, (although, the student may still have to pay to use these facilities), and room cleaning. Some include pre-paid meal plans.

- Go on an accommodation tour. Have a look at as much of the accommodation being shown as you can. Most universities will allow you to go into some of the accommodation on a tour to have a proper look at what you will be paying for. Note: this will only happen on the open days.

- The finance meeting will explain all the financial side of things. The loans, bursaries and all other incentives. Look into all of this carefully and maximise out on what you are entitled to. There is plenty of literature to back up what you hear. I say this as it is A LOT to take in all at once and so it is nice to know that you can find out any information that you are not sure about.

- Ask about the security of the university and what they have in place for safety of the students. This might seem a bit of an odd thing to be thinking about, but it is important to consider as most want to go away from home to study. It just gives you peace of mind when you know the university takes safety seriously, (and most do take it very seriously). If their students feel safe this makes the whole experience much more pleasant. It is one thing less for them to contend with when leaving home.

Our child was no exception. She didn't go locally to university, so she was going to live away from home, and when that happens security becomes more poignant. You should qualify the university from a safety aspect because it is important.

We were impressed with the university that our daughter chose. It had a connection with a cab company. This helped with two points: firstly, they knew the cab company was safe, and secondly, there was the facility that if the student didn't have any money or enough money with them they had a tab situation that could be sorted out later. Students used their student card and it was paid off at another time. It had an on-campus security guard system which makes sure no one makes too much noise, that students in their first year who have drunk too much get home to their accommodation safely and that everyone is safe on campus. They also had a facility called 'Nightline', where students could call up someone on a given number and talk to them if they thought they were being followed, if they had forgotten their door key, if they were ill, or someone else was ill, and they were not sure what to do about it. All very impressive facilities that make you, as a parent, feel more confident that, if a negative situation arose, there were procedures in place to deal with most eventualities. Now these things are not necessarily what you think about initially when you are looking at a university and they are not essential to picking a university of course, but they do make the experience for parents and students much easier.

- Your child may need to work whilst being a student at university. So look into what the uni has in place for this to be achievable. Some universities do offer employment on campus, but to be successful in finding work on campus they will need to be quick off the mark. These jobs can go within a few days or even hours. For the best chance they need to look into what jobs are on offer, where to look for them and when they are advertised.

Jobs that may be on offer are: Student Ambassadors, Student Helpers (employed in a variety of casual tasks, such as arrivals days, open days and events), Student Callers (interviewed and trained to conduct short telephone campaigns and surveys on behalf of the University), Student Demonstrators (to conduct lab or classroom demonstration sessions), Union bar staff, onsite shop staff, Fresher's temporary staff.

Be aware that although most universities are quite happy for their students to find work they do not advise more than 16-20 hours a week as they feel any more than this could impact on their university course.

- Some courses include a year where the student studies or works abroad as part of the degree. If their course is one of these you will need to look into this in detail. Erasmus covers the year abroad in Europe.

It is a European student exchange scheme, but there are also other abroad options such as in the USA, Canada or elsewhere. Check with the university to see what they provide.

- Although they won't need this initially, it is a good idea to find out what links the university has with employers/companies for the future. This is important because you want to feel that the university is able to help with employment when they have finished the degree. Also look into what internship programmes the university runs. An internship provides the opportunity to enhance their employability by applying their skills in a professional context, enhancing their CV and obtaining relevant experience for them for their future.

- Ask about the local area. By this I don't mean on campus, I mean the closest town to where they will be going to university. Ask the students about it. If they like it, how easy is it to get to? Any information that they think is of interest or is relevant to you.

Whilst you are on your university 'checking out day', if you get the chance it is well worth going into the local area and having a look around to get a feel of what it is like and to see if you like it. This gives you all peace of mind that the area is of a standard that you would expect and feel happy with. This is especially important if it is a small campus and the majority of facilities are in the town; similarly, it is important if the university is particularly close to the town, because there is a good chance your child will spend a lot of time there.

- Enquire about the university transport and what it is like. Some universities are very well set up for transport, with busses to the nearest town and providing students with a student bus pass/ticket deal.
- What activities do they have on site for fun? Is there a bar, club, gym?
- Find out about the student union, which may run a large number of clubs and societies to help the students settle in and become part of areas which interest them, giving them a wider aspect of university life. They give support by representing students on issues that they feel strongly about and provide commercial services such as running the bars, clubs and gigs held at the university. They also offer advice on areas such as financial, housing and academic appeals if you have any worries.

If you are unable to either get to an open day or do a self-tour, you can do a virtual tour of the universities of your choices and look up as much information as possible on their websites, which are usually very informative. Many of them do virtual tours of the accommodation as well so that you can get a good feel as to what is on offer. But it is important not to rely on a virtual tour if at all possible, because, try as it might, the virtual tour cannot capture the atmosphere of the real place. Even if it looks fantastic on a virtual tour, when going to the university itself, you may find that it isn't the place for your child.

Once you have made your choices of universities there is an opportunity for the applicants to view the university on a visit day. If you have missed the open days and not been able to do a self-tour I would recommend that you go to the visit day so you can see where you may be going to. These are really good and are along the same lines as an open day. There is lots of information available, so you should be able to catch up on most of what you missed on the initial open day.

7

Cutting the list

Now the next phase is another bizarre exercise. You have to shorten the list down to five universities. After you have visited all the universities that you want to go and look at, you have cut this list down to five, and the list is sent with the initial application to UCAS before the deadline (which, if you remember, may be different days depending on where you are applying to). With our application we put in a mixed bag of universities for the five choices. This was to give us some elbow-room with the final decision. The top three were aspirational universities and the other two were back up choice universities that we liked. This gave us some flexibility, depending on the exam results. One word of advice is to make sure you use all five choices.

This then has to be downsized to two at the end of the exercise! "What? How does that work?" I hear you ask. Well this is another university oddity. The idea behind this is that your charge i.e. the one who will be going to uni, may not receive an offer of a place from all five of their university choices, hence me advising you to apply to all your five options. Applying to all five gives some leverage when deciding where to go. We heard of some people that only got offered places at one or two universities. If this happens then having the opportunity to choose five places initially is a good thing. However, at the other end of the spectrum if you get offered all five places it then becomes very difficult, as you have to discard three perfectly good places. Even worse, if you don't get the required entrance grades for the universities that you have chosen to go to, some of the original five that you had to turn down you may now be looking at trying to get into through Clearing.

Clearing is UCAS's process that lets you apply for courses that still have places vacant. This is available if the track status says 'You are in Clearing' or 'Clearing has started'. Even if you didn't get the required grades your application may be under consideration by the university if the status has not been updated. It is worth ringing the university to see what your situation is, so you know what action to take next. You are also able to use Clearing if you retract your application to your firm and/or insurance choices, but consult your advisors before going down this route. Clearing opens on results day and remains open until late September. You can find all available courses online. Once a shortlist has been made of courses you are interested in you should call the universities. It is important that your child phones up the university and not you. They will need their Clearing number, which they can find on UCAS Track, and their personal ID number. Make sure they have their A level, GCSE grades and UCAS points value to hand. Initially they will be talking to a Clearing helpline member who will talk about their results. They will then be passed on to a course administrator to see if they meet the requirements. This is a mini-interview, so they need to make sure they do their research beforehand. They need to promote themselves and explain why they wish to do the course.

I haven't got any firsthand experience of Clearing. We were fortunate enough not to have to go down that route. This seems another odd university avenue that can add extra stress. However, people who have used Clearing seemed to be well looked after, and most get places that they are satisfied with.

If you do need to go through the Clearing process all the previous work that you did by looking at universities suddenly becomes very useful, and having previously chosen the five options is now an advantage. If you have to go through Clearing once you get your results, you now may know which Clearing places you want to apply for. This can help get Clearing out of the way more quickly, and it can mean that you get a place where others who don't know which Clearing place to go to might not. Clearing is essentially a race to get all university places filled up. There is some good news in this: universities do want to get all the places they have filled up. So they will still try to get you to go to their university, if they can. An added advantage when you've gone around the universities that you're applying to through Clearing is that you know exactly where you're going to end up.

This is a good point to write about the second choice that you get in the UCAS application. Once the five universities have come back to you, this is when to decide which two universities you are most interested in. Option two, then, becomes a back up option. You still apply for accommodation in option two, and you still get information from them right up until you get your results, and your top university decides whether or not to let you in. It is probably worth picking a higher entry level university for your first choice, (if that is your favourite university), and then picking a slightly lower entry level university for your second choice, so that it acts like a cushion option. If your top university doesn't let you in, the second choice university still might. If this happens, you don't have to go through Clearing, and you would attend and be a member of your second choice university as though it was your first choice.

8

Accommodation

When they have chosen their final two university options they also need to find out when the accommodation needs to have been selected by.

Some universities give conditional or unconditional offers. Basically, unconditional means you should get your choice of accommodation, and conditional means you should get your choice if you get the grades the university requires for you to do the course. Even then, whether or not they get accommodation can still be dependent on how far away you live from campus. Also, even an unconditional offer might not mean you will get your first choice of accommodation – it just means you will definitely be given accommodation in halls of residence somewhere.

So while disregarding the three perfectly good university places, you also need to think about accommodation in the two universities that you have chosen. It is at this point that you need to inform the university which of the accommodation you would like to have and in which order of preference you would like the choice to be in.

Most of the universities give you a choice of two accommodations: your preferred choice and a back up. The choices are different university to university; however, most of the combinations involve the following: rooms in flats, rooms in houses and rooms in colleges/faculties. Some will have en-suites, some will have shared bathrooms and some will have a washbasin in the room. Most have some sort of kitchen, which is usually shared. The number of people a kitchen is shared between can vary. Some universities also provide options for catering such as bed and breakfast or bed and evening meal. The virtual tour can be helpful when choosing accommodation choices at this stage as it can help as a reminder of what it is like. If you have visited the accommodation when you have been to the university this is obviously very helpful. Once the choices have been made you won't need to do any more until the results are through and you have made the final choice as to which university you actually want to go to.

Accommodation choices come down to what criterion are important to you. Is money the most important factor? Do you want to be on campus or off campus? This might depend on what the city is like near the campus. Do you mind sharing and if so with how many? Is an en-suite important or are you happy to share a bathroom? All of these things are important, but are obviously different for everyone.

Some essential things to know about campus renting are that most utilities are usually included in the rent. However be aware that some things are not included such as washing machines. You will have a contractual agreement that will specify the length of time your student rental contract lasts. Check your contract to see whether you are able to leave your items in your room for the full year, or if you have to clear your room because someone else will be staying there during holiday periods.

Our criteria were based on the accommodation having an en-suite, and a reasonable price. As not all accommodation has en-suites, this narrowed the options we had and led to our daughter being off campus, but only very slightly. Be prepared to pay more for an en-suite. Her room/flat was just across the road from the university campus. This actually became an advantage as she felt that she actually left the university at the end of the day, giving her a distinction between work and home. Had she been on-site it may have felt monotonous. As it was, it gave her a bit of breathing space, but was not too far removed that she felt separated from the university. Her flat was in a purpose-built estate owned by the university. There was a whole area of flat blocks full of students, so, although slightly off the campus, it still felt completely part of it. In her flat she shared a kitchen with eight people. This sounds like a lot, but it was a decent size kitchen with two fridges and two freezers. It had adequate cupboard space and a table and chairs big enough for everyone to eat around. This was excellent as they all got to know each other in the flat and could eat properly together, if they so wished. This became quite a social area on occasions. They even celebrated certain events in the kitchen and it became a good meeting place for them all. However, they were also able to escape to their rooms with their own bathroom facilities when they wanted to.

The room was fairly basic, but perfectly sufficient. She had a single bed with the ability to pull it up, so that the space beneath the bed could be used for more storage. There was a large desk with shelves above it for books and more storage. The en-suite had a shower, sink and toilet. It was very cleverly designed. There was also a large hanging wardrobe with some high shelves. So everything was thought of for the first year students: not too big to overwhelm them, but just enough to make it useable and comfortable.

Another nice convenience that my daughter's uni provided was a cleaner. She would empty the student's bins and vacuum over the corridors outside their rooms. Twice a week she would clean the kitchen (no mean feat, and their kitchen was good compared to some), and once a week she would clean their bathrooms. They were expected to keep their rooms clean and tidy and keep on top of their washing up in the kitchen (quite right, too). This was no small task whilst sharing with a lot of other people. Some interesting habits start to materialise over time: things like once they had run out of their own crockery and cutlery they would use anyone else's that was around and clean. I was worried about the arguments that might have arisen from this, but my daughter's flat of eight people were all quite relaxed and they seemed to make it work. There was a bit of flexibility with freezer sharing space and milk-purchasing and borrowed items were always returned… eventually. So it was all good.

The cleaner was obviously paid for in the price of the accommodation, but I found out later that this had hidden benefits that I hadn't put in the equation originally. As I said, she came into their rooms to empty their bins daily. Whilst doing this she actually kept a bit of an eye of them all in the flats. Firstly when emptying the bins she made sure they were at least *compos mentis* to a certain degree! This is not as silly as it sounds as we all know that in many cases university is an initiation of alcohol, and even the most modest before they go to uni will experiment whilst there. My daughter's cleaner was a lovely lady who had got the balance completely correct; not overly interested to be in their way, but keeping tabs on them to make sure they were ticking along fine.

Overall, the first year accommodation was a very positive experience.

9

Facts to note

There are a few things that you need to be aware of:

- Make sure you are home and *not on holiday* when the A Level results are released. This will happen sometime in mid-August. Check with the school when the results are due out. This is extremely important, as it may all be straightforward if they have got their place, but if they didn't they need to be near a phone to call Clearing and organise a new place if they still want to go to university. This needs to have some time dedicated to it, as it can be quite time-consuming. As you can imagine, the people you are trying to contact are in demand at this point and the phones can be very busy. Even if it all goes well, it is nice to be able to be together to talk and organise the next phases that will be coming. This can be a very exciting point and a great time for celebration.
- Have all relevant websites to hand: the UCAS website for tracking the situation and placement

announcements; the university websites which you want to get into.

- Have all the relevant telephone numbers ready to call: the UCAS telephone number for Clearing if that situation occurs; the university telephone numbers if it is unclear on the UCAS website.

- Once they have confirmed their university place by phoning them you need to be around when the university try to contact your child to tell them what accommodation they will be offered. This will all happen around the same time, in August, as when they get their results and accept their university place. Note that accommodation is sorted out about a week after the place is confirmed on the course! Make sure your child is at home to receive this call or email, because if they miss it they may not get the choice of accommodation they would like. Your child is going to spend their first year there so it is important to get the best possible offer for their living quarters. The university will then be able to tell them when they can move into the accommodation. This is usually just before Freshers' Week, which is normally a week or two weeks before university tuition begins.

10

Practicalities

Before they go to uni there are some practicalities that need to be covered with them. They need to become adults very quickly when they go. From being loved and cherished at home they will be expected to stand on their own two feet at university. With this in mind it is our responsibility to assist with this journey for them to make it as easy and painless as possible. Some of the things that I found really helpful for our daughter were quite basic, but made a real difference to her adjustment.

You/they will need to open a student bank account. This is very important, as they need to have the capability of being in control of their own finances. They need to have a facility for their loans/grants to be sent to them and any other income they have. They will need to be able to pay their bills for their accommodation, and they will need to have a bank account that is set up to be able to deal with this. Most student bank accounts come with a 0% overdraft. Our daughter's was £1000.00, but this may vary depending on the bank. Also make sure that they are aware that if they go over the overdraft limit the fines are hefty so they should avoid this! We always said to our daughter that if she was in a bit of a mess monetary-wise it was much better to call us sooner rather than later so that we could sort it out before it got out of hand.

You may also need to send them money. As they are expected to be grown up as soon as they are off to university, they sometimes feel under pressure to do it all correctly and often this just doesn't happen. We told our daughter not to leave it too late before saying anything, but if she did forget, to not hide the problem and just to let us know. They are, after all, still learning about supporting themselves and living on their own. If they do get into financial difficulty, just deal with it as soon as is possible and don't make a big thing about it, otherwise they may not come to you in the future and this could be a far worse situation to have to sort out.

Opening a student bank account sounds straightforward, and it is once you get to grips with it. Again the Internet has made it all just that bit easier: punch in 'student bank accounts' and have a look to see what is on offer. Most of the major banks offer student accounts, as you would imagine they would; they obviously want to catch the next generation of customers early. They are fully aware that if they give them a good start in the banking experience they could have them as customers for life, or a good proportion of it anyway. With this in mind they all give incentives so it is worth finding out what the incentives are and why you should seriously think of setting up the student bank account with them.

One thing which you might not immediately think of when looking into student accounts is whether they will be able to access their student bank easily. If the bank does not have a branch near the uni that you have chosen it is probably better to go to a different student account provider. It is nice if they have any queries or worries to be able to go straight into the bank and just ask. Don't be enticed by one that hasn't got a branch nearby, as they will have to phone the bank if they have any queries. When we looked into how much these phone calls would cost, they were not cheap. We all know how long and difficult it can be to get hold of the people we need to speak to if we have a problem. You don't want your child to have to deal with that situation.

Also check how long interest-free rates last with their student bank account after they graduate. They may have to re-think their bank account at this point. Bear in mind most banks will want to keep their customers who were students so they may have some good options for them if they need to upgrade their account at this point.

You/they may also want to consider a student credit card, which can be done with the same provider that you set up the student bank account with. This is a good idea too because if they are purchasing things from the internet such as books or stationary or food this is a safer way to do it, rather than using their student bank details. You will probably have to teach them how the credit card works, so all the basics have to be covered to stop them getting into financial trouble. Our daughter set her credit balance to be paid off automatically on a monthly basis, therefore stopping her ever getting any charges. This is obviously not always possible, but then the basic monthly payment should at least be explained to avoid any issues arising in the future unnecessarily.

It might be worth you thinking about opening an interest-free payment credit card to give you more flexibility to help them out with any cash flow problems. It can be useful for things such as the deposit for where they are living until they get their maintenance loan money through. These usually last for twelve-fifteen months at 0%. Make sure that once this period has finished you close the credit card, as it will have finished its 0% period and open a new one with someone else, if it has been useful. If you are doing this be aware that it can take quite a long time to set the card up. Sometimes it can take a month to get the credit card through.

Teach them how to read bills. They won't need this so much in the first year, although they will need to pay the university for their accommodation, but it is still important that they recognise what a bill looks like, that they realise they have to pay their bills and know how and when to do this.

In the second year when our daughter was renting a house with her housemates they all had to play a part in paying the house bills. They seemed to do it very amicably as they had learned how to read and pay bills in their first year. One person paid one bill, another paid another and so on. If done this way, one person doesn't end up with an enormous sum to pay out, and then wait for the rest of the housemates to pay up. Paying it one bill each means that you can be pretty sure the cheques won't bounce. They always paid by cheque, which enabled them not to give anyone their bank details. This was thought to be the right thing to do so that when they left their rental house their banking details were not on any utility services computer database.

Teach them how to food-shop and cook before they go to uni. 'Really?' you say. I know this sounds like I'm taking it all to the extreme, but this was one of the things I did which was well worth the effort and my daughter can now shop for food and cook food properly. I, because of this knowledge, can rest at night knowing that she is all ok in that respect.

So, give them lessons in cookery. You might not feel you are competent in teaching them to cook, but even if you aren't great yourself, they are going to be worse and any instruction that you can give them will help. I was amazed at how some of the students didn't even know how to cook basic foods. Even teaching baked beans on toast and scrambled egg, both of which are cheap meals but full of nutrition, would be a real help to them. In fact, eggs are a very good basic food to teach them how to cook. They are the original fast food, too. They can make soft-boiled eggs for dippy eggs, hard-boiled eggs for egg mayonnaise sandwiches, scrambled eggs, fried eggs with bacon or sausages and omelette. So many dishes, which can be made quickly and cheaply.

The summer before you pack them off and potentially never see them again, (only joking, they'll be back to get their washing done), it is a good idea to teach them how to shop as well as cook. 'How to shop'? I hear you laugh. 'They don't need lessons there'. Well actually, some of them do. Some of them don't know about savvy shopping and they will need this when they go to uni, even if money is not too much of an issue. Teach them about the supermarkets. No doubt most of them will just use the same supermarkets that their parents use and this is fine, but it is well worth widening their views as not all supermarkets may be available where they are going to uni. Teach them how to shop so they don't waste money. Some of the budget supermarkets are very good value and good quality. These may come in useful when they are at uni. Teach them how to shop carefully; by this I mean when choosing fruit and vegetables, make sure they pick up good quality food and not food that may turn bad quickly.

Teach them about hygiene. Sounds basic, but I have heard some horror stories that would make your toes curl! Students can be a bit of a nightmare when it comes to hygiene. This is because their mothers have been cleaning up after them for the last eighteen years! Again, you can start this process off in the summer holidays before they go to uni. They will need to learn how to do the following things:

- Washing up and drying
- Washing and drying clothes. Washing the tea towel and dish-cloth on a regular basis. I make this point as I heard a terrible story about a friend's daughter in her first year at uni. Apparently when she went to collect the daughter on one of the holidays she asked her daughter who the tea towels belonged to? They didn't know. No one recognised them. The mother took the tea towels home in a bag, as they looked a

positively disgusting brownish-green colour. When she took them home she boil washed them twice and to her surprise they came out white! Her daughter then said, 'Oh yes I remember them, I'd forgotten they were that colour!'

- Vacuuming
- Ironing (not much of this will be done, but it is still a good opportunity to teach them)
- Washing bathrooms, including toilets (remind them about mould removal)
- Dusting
- Mopping floors (they probably won't need this in the first year, but they might do thereafter)

They won't do most of this when at uni, but if they are taught then at least they will know how to do the important bare minimum.

Two other tips I would recommend is to tell them to take perishables out of their plastic packaging when putting it in the fridge. Students will probably not eat these types of foods quickly and if left in plastic they may sweat and deteriorate quicker. Also it is worth pointing out to them, for when they are coming home, that emptying the fridge and taking the rubbish bins out is a good idea – otherwise they may have some pretty horrible situations to contend with when they get back to uni. They may have to deal with solid milk and maggots if they don't keep up these basic jobs.

Start thinking about what they are going to need at uni. This should be a list that you can add to at any time. Don't leave this to the last minute – remember they are leaving home and setting up house, so they need all the bits you needed when you did this. This was my very first list and, believe me, it was added to! Saucepans, plates, bowls, cutlery, glasses, mugs, kitchen utensils, oven gloves, tea towel, dish cloth, scrubber, airier for clothes, towels, bedding, washing powder, conditioner, colour catchers, basic cleaning products.

Buy a 16-25 railcard for them. This saves them a 1/3rd off their train tickets when they buy them in advance on a student price. Also if you shop at Tesco's and save Clubcard points you can use your Clubcard points to buy the 16-25 railcard for them which saves you the cost of buying the card. Depending where they go to uni they might be doing a lot more travelling to and from home so this can be a very worthwhile purchase.

You have some research to do now. You will need to find out how and where they should make the journeys between uni and home. I mention this because some of the journeys are not straightforward. There can be several changes on route. You will need to check out what the prices of the trips to university and back are so you know where you stand before they go. These can also vary depending on the times of travel. Don't forget to use the student railcard; it does make a difference and is definitely worth it. Note that advanced booking of train tickets on the internet is cheaper.

Buy a student Oyster card if they are going to university in London. You can only get this organised when they have actually started university, as they need their university number for this, but as soon as they know they are going this can be organised.

Homesickness is something that is often an afterthought. You may have been so busy with all the fundamentals that the psychological aspect can quite easily get forgotten. The bottom line, though, is that they may be homesick when they go to uni, especially if they are a long way from home.

It is surprising how the build-up and the excitement of everything can carry you along for quite a time. But once they are dropped off and you have helped them settle in it's just, well, a shock. They may in the first few weeks feel quite isolated and out of their depth.

Get social media set up. Skype was absolutely excellent for all of us. We were worried about her and wanted to make sure she was ok, but without it seeming like we were overly protective. She did, surprisingly, feel quite homesick initially and it enabled her to speak to us whenever she wanted to, which helped. Also if she needed to ask us anything, which she did a lot in the first few weeks, it was easy to do and felt more real as we could see her. I would recommend this even for the ones who don't have the problem of homesickness. It's good to touch base with them every now and then, even if you are just making sure they are ok.

Their habits change when they have been at uni for a bit. Although this is not an immediate process it does happen. They become more nocturnal, late nights and late mornings become usual. The other bonus of Skype was checking up on her and how she actually looked. I remember speaking to her once and she looked absolutely awful. If I had been speaking to her on the phone I would never have known this, but seeing her on my computer when Skyping it was perfectly obvious that she was not getting enough sleep. We were able to have a conversation about this and then check up on her to make sure that she was looking better. As I said, Skype was a Godsend, and I would highly recommend for everyone to seriously consider it.

11

Teaching them how to cook!
The cook section, tips and techniques

I was amazed at how different they all were in the way of food. Some of them were quite good and some of them had clearly never been shown anything in the kitchen at home before at all! Some of them came up with the most amazingly bizarre eating habits for lunch and dinners. They all did it differently, but over a period of time they learnt from each other, taking some points to heart and discarding the things that they weren't going to use because quite frankly, they were just a little bit strange.

There are some things that they may need to be taught. For instance it is important to teach them some money-saving traits. A really good way of saving money and for them to eat proper meals is to show them that if they buy fresh meat in family packs and then freeze the meat individually they can defrost one portion of meat daily to have a good meal. This saves money too because the meat is bought in bulk. As long as the meat was frozen properly they had meals to last them for as long as they left them in the freezer. However, if you are going to do this you have to teach them how to defrost the meat safely too. I always advised my daughter to get out what meat she wanted the night before and defrost it on a plate or in a bowl overnight. In the morning pop it in the fridge on the plate or in the bowl and then cook it later that evening. By giving the meat a good 12 hours at room temperature to defrost they can be sure that the meat was safe, but make sure it is put in the fridge after the initial twelve hours so that it keeps nicely.

Teach them other habits you use. All the things that you do automatically, well, they aren't automatic to students. So impart that information. It will help them and others too. A very basic example was my daughter had a flat-mate who had bought an onion. Because she didn't know that she didn't have to cook the whole onion she ate it all in one meal. Once she was told that most vegetables could be put in the fridge even once started, just put a bit of kitchen roll over the cut part, she saved time, money and didn't force herself to eat something unnecessarily. She saved time because she wasn't doing so much shopping, and money because instead of one meal she got several meals from one onion. A small and obvious practice, but well worth its weight in gold to a student. So have a think about any tips and techniques that you use at home on a regular basis without even thinking about it and pass those little gems on. You won't realise what a difference those insights will make to them.

Ideas for meals

- Baked beans on toast
- Scrambled eggs on toast
- Soft-boiled eggs with toast
- Fried egg with bacon or sausage (or both)
- Omelette and salad
- Baked potatoes with cheese/ baked beans/ Bolognese sauce/ chilli con carnie sauce/ tuna & salad cream/ chicken curry
- Sausages with mash and peas, or with salad and jacket potato
- Bacon, egg, chips and beans
- Spaghetti Bolognese
- Tuna pasta bake
- Fish and chips
- Cornish pasties with salad and chips/jacket potato or with vegetable and chips/jacket potato
- Sausage rolls with salad and chips/jacket potato or with vegetables and chips/jacket potato
- Cheese rolls with chips
- Salad – tuna, egg, cheese & ham with bread/crusty rolls
- Pizza and salad
- Meat:
  Chicken – baked in the oven or stir fried with salad, such as Caesar salad. You can also make a casserole with packet sauces such as curry
  Turkey – grilled/ stir fried/ with sauces
  Pork – grilled, stir fried/ casserole
  Mince – Bolognese/ chilli con carnie/ Shepherd's pie

Meat balls – with tomato sauce and rice or with Penne pasta, broccoli and gravy

Food shopping for them

Everyone does things differently. Some parents give their children a supermarket card and top it up monthly. Some people put a monthly amount into their child's bank account. Some people take their children back to uni and stock them up with food and some people do a mixture of all!

This is a typical shopping list that we would buy for our daughter at the beginning of term. This was rather a large exercise, but this food was bought to last for the majority of the twelve-week term and all she would have to do is buy her perishables on a weekly basis.

- Chicken breast, pork loin, turkey, breaded turkey steak, mincemeat, sausages, bacon, meatballs, hot dogs, pies, sausage rolls
- Fish fingers, tinned tuna
- Ham
- Milk, butter, cheese, yogurt, eggs
- Salad, vegetables, fruit, red onion
- Frozen vegetables – peas/sweet corn/mixed carrots, broccoli
- Pasta, rice, Chinese noodles, tortilla wraps, pizza
- Cereals, bread
- Tomato puree, tinned tomato's, baked beans, stir fry sauces, oil, salt

- Soup, curry sauce, tomato sauce, salad cream
- Crisps
- Tinned fruit
- Sweet snacks – biscuits, chocolate bars
- Fruit juice, hot chocolate, coffee
- Shower gel, shampoo, conditioner, tissues, toilet paper, cotton buds
- Food freezer bags, cling film, kitchen foil, kitchen towel, multi-purpose cloths.
- Toilet paper

12

Moving In

You've accepted the university place!
You've accepted the accommodation offered!
You've looked into when Freshers' week is!
You've looked into when you can move into your accommodation!

It is now time to think about everything that you are going to need to take to university for your child. How are you going to get all your things there? This is another exercise in which Mum and Dad are required to participate. You will be backwards and forwards bringing STUFF, far too much STUFF, to and from uni on roughly a semester rotation in the first year. You have to decide when you are going to take it all to university. Usually they are allowed to move into their accommodation just before Freshers' week starts. This is a good way of getting them settled into student/ university life as quickly and as painlessly as possible.

Moving all their gear is no mean feat. They are leaving home and setting up their own lives, so all the things you do when you buy your first little place is basically along the same lines as what is required here. They need clothes (obviously), food (obviously), kitchen utensils, pots and pans, crockery, glasses, bedding, a clothes airier, household cleaning products like washing powder and washing up liquid. They don't, however, need dishwasher tablets like my daughter asked for… I told her with a smile that she wouldn't need these as she would be washing up all her dirty dishes by hand from now on at uni – she would therefore be needing a tea towel ☺. They need personal products like shampoo, soap and whatever else they usually use when they are living at home – in bucket loads. They will need preferably their own PC, stationary, and a printer is helpful. It is a huge exercise and needs to have thought and consideration used in carrying it out.

Then you, as parents, need to organise the logistics of this: how you actually get all their gear to university. We are very fortunate as we have a motorhome, which was extremely useful in moving everything into the accommodation. Our daughter does not move lightly. You might laugh, but she actually managed to fill up our six-berth motorhome when she moved in. I will say the faces of other parents when we turned up in it is a picture that will stay with me for quite some time.

Once you have decided when you are taking them and have bought all the necessary items for them to start their uni life it all becomes quite straightforward. You just need to get them to their university, unpack them and help them settle in a bit. Tea is a good idea at this point. Not necessarily for the student, but for the parents, it helps a lot. It gives you something to do whilst they are looking at the mountains of stuff that they have brought with them and whilst they are deciding where they are going to put it all in their tiny new room. For any assistance that they need you are still on hand, but they have a bit of space to think about what they need to do next. Surprisingly our daughter managed to get everything in her tiny room. I was extremely impressed with the design. It was perfect for someone starting a new adventure. It fitted in perfectly with her new lifestyle, but wasn't too big that it became overwhelming.

Once this has all been done it is time for parents to depart. This is quite a surreal moment. You have been working towards this for weeks. You knew it was coming and now it is actually here. It's time to say goodbye. It's time to let them sort themselves out from here on in. It feels weird. You stand around awkwardly waiting for the right moment to say your goodbyes without really wanting to go. You know it is that time and it has to be done. So goodbyes are said, and good lucks are too, and then you drive off feeling like something is missing. All of a sudden everything feels a bit flat and like they are changing forever, but you also know that is the way it is supposed to be. So, with an empty seat in the vehicle that you came to deliver them in, you trek back home hoping that they will be happy, the course will be what they thought it would be, they will make nice friends and that they will do well.

Now this is something that I am going to warn you about. We were warned about it by my sister-in-law, but really took it only tongue in cheek. Something that you will not have put into the equation probably over the very busy last few weeks as you were so busy running around getting your daughter/son ready for their adventure. You, as parents have to be aware that at some point this is when realisation starts to kick in. It is a very exciting time for everyone, but also it is a big thing. Make no mistake about that. It can catch you off guard that actually, this is a momentous time for your child and you as parents. They are moving on with their lives. So be prepared for the moment when this penny drops, as it probably will do even if you are the most together and composed parent. But remember, you have spent the last eighteen years loving, nurturing, guiding and advising them for this end in sight.

For us it was not the day that we dropped her off at uni; it was actually the evening before that it hit us. Our motorhome was packed up and ready to go. We had dinner and there was nothing left for us to do until we actually took her the following day. There was NOTHING left for us to do. What we had been working towards was now here and *that's* when the full impact hit us… So after a big cry and cuddle we felt better, but it was a very sad moment for us all. However, as well as being sad, it was also an exciting time; there were lots of mixed emotions. The next morning we all got up with purpose, and focussed on getting her to uni as quickly and painlessly as possible.

If you aren't that type of parent, please just ignore the above couple of paragraphs. But beware, it is surprising how it can affect you, and most parents *are* affected by it.

Once at uni there is some protocol that has to be followed, some things that have to be done. Firstly, you have to tell the university that you have arrived. They will give you lots of information about where things are and events that they are supposed to attend, such as Freshers' events and welcome talks. They will also tell you where their accommodation is and how to get there. You will be told where to collect the key for their flat/room so that you can make your way to it when you are ready.

Then you have to find the accommodation. Usually there are lots of student helpers around to give you directions and help you take their gear into their accommodation. A couple of tips I would advise at this point: once you have been shown to their room and you get your bearings, go into the kitchen area, as most will be sharing this in their first year. Get them to choose a shelf in the fridge, freezer and cupboard spaces as quickly as possible and put their name on them somehow with a label or tape a piece of paper with their name on it onto the cupboard; if you don't do this they will be stuck with what is left and they will have to live with that for the whole year.

After this, all they need to do is unpack their baggage. We went to the local supermarket and bought enough food to last for twelve weeks; by this I mean dry food, such as pasta, rice, crisps, biscuits and anything else that we could think of that would be needed. We bought meat and fish which she was instructed how to pack up individually in freezer bags so that she could defrost a meal's worth to eat at a time. We instructed her how to defrost safely and how long food could last before it was unsafe to eat and had to be disposed of. We also bought her perishables: bread, vegetables, salad and fruit, but this would have to be topped up by herself as and when.

So, once she had been delivered and we had done the shopping, it was time for us to go. We needed to leave her and let her get on with unpacking and settling in properly. It was time to say goodbye and good luck.

13

Freshers' Week commences

Freshers' Week normally starts the week or two weeks before university lectures begin. As Freshers' Week begins your child will probably be feeling excited and nervous. Below is some advice parents could give their charges, and some things for them to be aware of:

- The people they will be sharing accommodation with don't have to be their lifetime friends.
- Take it easy. Some universities' Freshers' Week goes on for fourteen days! That's a fortnight spent celebrating or socialising by a lot of young people, and most will be living away from home for the first time. Tell them not to overdo it. They need to keep up their sleep and remember to eat food.
- Make sure they budget appropriately. Budgeting will be a steep learning curve, but learning what they need to spend on food, going out and items to study will allow them to enjoy ten to twelve weeks as opposed to just one to two.
- Don't miss out on the Freshers' Fairs, which is where

students can join societies and clubs that interest them within the university. Most will go to at least one or two societies, so they should get a feel for the kind of people they want to socialise with, as well as the activity.

- Missing home is to be expected. No one admits it, but missing parents, siblings and home is normal, and there are a few students who drop out every year after a few weeks because they aren't ready to leave home. Balance is the best way to avoid homesickness: tell them to keep in touch and talk to them at least a couple of times a week. Advise them to talk to new friends about home life. More than likely they will be going through the same thing.

- Non-drinking Freshers. They should be aware they are not alone. Student unions have become aware of this situation and are now considering hosting alcohol-free events. Every university has faith societies such as Christian, Jewish and Muslim societies representing different beliefs. They don't have to feel like they should spend time with people who are always intoxicated. There is always someone like-minded in the mass.

- Be wary of student politics. They should enrol into their ranks only if they are enthusiastic and committed.

- Be responsible. They have to start to understand that they are an adult now, so they need to make sure they have paid the rent, have food in, they can access the university library etc. In week two, when tutors start to give their work out, this will be very useful. They need to keep their accommodation in a reasonable condition. Cleaning dishes, clothes, and keeping a tidy room will keep new friends happy and accommodating.

- Enjoy it, but if it isn't your thing don't worry about it. It isn't everyone's best week of their lives.

14

Student Life begins – Year One

The next few weeks are critical. It is a good idea to be in contact with your daughter/son on a fairly regular basis. Some of them don't want to do this; they just want to go to uni and be on their way. Others, however, need parent contact to help with the homesickness side of things and settling in. Bear in mind they are now managing their finances, their shopping, their cooking, their studies, their house cleaning, and their life all on their own. Don't forget only a few weeks previously they were still at home. So being in contact at this point is good from all of that point of view. It gives everyone peace of mind.

Once they are settled in and you know they are happy with everything i.e. they like the university, they like the course and lecturers, they like the people, they like the socialising, then things start to settle down and you won't need to be on social media or skype as often.

There were some unusual habits that appeared after time. I noticed that they became almost nocturnal. They started to have naps in the afternoon so that they could cope with their nightlife! Some of these new habits were completely different from how they would behave at home. There were a few occasions when we Skyped our daughter, and to be honest, she looked pretty awful. She had clearly not had enough sleep and she just looked exhausted. However, after a few more weeks these new habits became less frequent and they appeared to be much more content and able to cope with their new lifestyle.

By the time Christmas begins to loom, life has pretty much regained some normality. But then, bizarrely, after Christmas was the time at my daughter's university where they had to start looking for their digs for the second year! I was quite shocked at this. I couldn't help thinking that we have only just sorted out everything for her to enjoy in the first year, and yet now she already had to look into sorting out where she was going to be living in her second year! Note: this doesn't happen this early at all universities.

Most universities only provide accommodation for the first year. This is due to limited availability. For the subsequent years the student has to sort out their own accommodation. However, most universities do help with this by offering housing advice. They may have meetings to start pointing the students in the right direction for their research of their second year accommodation. This is usually the best and safest way to find your next student accommodation/home. They may be able to offer contract advice and respond to specific housing queries too, or put you in contact with someone who can help. Sometimes they will provide a free House Hunting Guide or hold up-to-date listings of available accommodation throughout the year. They may also host Housing Socials to help students meet prospective housemates. Most students will have to find private accommodation for themselves, but there is normally quite a bit of help on hand.

Something to take into consideration when looking for accommodation is the distance from the university and the local town/city. Does the area benefit from good bus links? How far is it from the local shops, takeaways etc.

There are quite significant differences between accommodation in student residences and living in the private sector:

- Most rooms are in houses that share bathroom facilities, although you will find some en-suite options. Rents vary depending on the size and condition of the rooms and the house.
- Utilities are not usually included in the rent, and residents are responsible for dealing with utility providers. As previously indicated, it is fairer to designate one resident's name per bill so that no one person is responsible for all the household bills. We advised that they didn't put down their bank details to the utility provider and just paid the bills by cheques. When the bill arrived they could split the amount between the number of people renting. However, some bed-sits and rooms with resident landlords do come inclusive of utilities.
- They will have a different type of contract, a tenancy agreement. The minimum length of the tenancy

agreement will be six months but ten, eleven or twelve-month agreements are most common for student accommodation. When you sign a contract, there will probably be some initial costs, such as agency fees and deposits. Most student accommodation will require a month rental deposit, a refundable deposit to cover any possible damage that may occur in the house. This could be one of the times when the 0% finance credit card may come in useful.

- Look out for joint tenancy contracts and not lead tenancy contracts. A joint tenancy contract means that everyone is responsible for their own part of the rental bill. If there is someone who doesn't pay their share the landlord should go after that person. A lead tenancy contract means that someone's name is the lead contact. They are the person responsible for everyone paying their part of the rental bill. If you do end up with one of these contracts try to avoid being the lead person.

It is thought that living in a student house is one of the defining experiences of student life. I would agree that it is part of the growing up process. Once they have to stand on their own two feet it is amazing how quickly they become adults in their own right.

Life as a student is now becoming established. Lectures and living away from home are becoming easier. A pattern is emerging. Student socialising starts to become more rounded and not so extreme. There are still blips every now and then, but staying in contact with your charge on a regular basis to touch base helps iron out these problems. If the settling-in period goes well, you are not required as much and you can feel happy that you have done your bit with the process of successfully installing your child into the university lifestyle.

From now on your role is much more basic. You are really only required to collect and take them back to the university on a termly basis and stock up their food quotas when they go back, so they can survive another term. This is pretty much all that is expected.

One thing we did make clear was that she was always welcome at home. If she wanted or needed to catch up with us she was only a train journey away, and we would be delighted for her to come home. This seemed to help in the first year as the need for home and family can be strong, and if they know that the hand of welcoming is always outstretched this helps them settle in.

15

A Year down the Line – Year Two

A year… a whole year! I know this because the friend of mine who organises the fund raiser 'belly dancing night', which I missed when the university search began, is asking if I would like to go again. So… I KNOW we are now a year down the line. This is how I know that I have misplaced a year of my life! Where did it go? Have I aged? I do feel a bit haggard and exhausted by the whole experience, but there is no visible evidence of this. However, I also know that it was a very worthwhile exercise for my daughter and a steep learning curve for us. I feel we have learnt a lot: some not so necessary life lessons, and some that will be useful for the future.

It has been a very successful first year. We have learnt that students can quite easily become nocturnal. Their eating habits are, to be perfectly honest, just odd on occasions. They do very strange things, but that is because they are basically teenagers pretending to be adults.

All in all the first year was successful. She enjoyed it

and was happy. So we were happy. All was good in our minds.

Now, once again we are off to take her back to university. This is the beginning of Year Two – but wait a minute, because it is slightly different this year. She is going to her very own student house, which she is sharing with two other students. We haven't really seen this house that she is renting; only a drive-by to see the outside after it was all organised. We did have a peek on Google maps just to make sure that it looked ok before she signed the joint tenancy contract though. I must say that we hadn't really been involved in it very much at all. This is how much they have grown up in that year.

She organised all this with the other two students she was sharing with. It was a little terraced house specially set up for student rental and already fully furnished. It was one of the houses on the university housing list. It was in a good area: half way between the university and the town with good bus links to both. Apparently they went to see quite a few houses. Some of them were pretty dismal, but this one was a gem. So they said that they wanted it almost as soon as they had seen it and spoken to the landlady's father, who was a very nice man. He explained the money side of it, the contract and all that was expected from them as well as what they should expect from the landlord in relation to the house. This was quite a quick turn-around due to the fact that the whole year of students are looking for somewhere to live at the same time, so the recommended student housing goes very quickly. Time is definitely off the essence!

My daughter's advice is, if you like a house, take it immediately so you don't lose it.

There are lots of different sorts and sizes of houses to rent too. Obviously they have to decide who they want to share with before choosing a house, and how many they are prepared to share with. Some houses are big and can take quite a number of students; these may have more than one bathroom. Some are small, like the terraced house that my daughter rented, and may have a room converted downstairs to take another student. This is a personal choice of what they feel comfortable with. Some like to be with lots of people and some prefer a smaller environment.

Make sure that you are happy with the contract that you will have to sign as their guardians. You have to sign just in case they falter with payments. You will be obliged contractually to pay if they don't for any reason. We spoke to the landlords before our daughter signed the contract. This was just to touch base with them and get a feel for the sort of people they were. This was a well worth exercise as it put our minds at rest and would make it easier in the future if we needed to speak to them.

Anyway, back to delivering our daughter for the second year at university. This was pretty straightforward this year. During the summer holiday our daughter had been assessing and accumulating everything which she would need to take back to uni so that by the time we were ready to take her back she had actually filled up our motorhome again! Clothes, food, household equipment, everything you could possibly imagine for setting up home. Note that not all student houses are furnished. If they are, they still might be missing some things – for example mirrors, bins, small store units etc.

So off we trundle to take her back. This felt different this year, not quite as tense, but just as exciting as we were going to see for the first time where she would be living. She was also excited as she hadn't seen it since they had agreed with the landlord that they were going to have it, and that was in the snow around Christmas time. So she was looking forward to seeing it again too and hoping that it was as good as she could remember it being.

We got there in good time and pulled up outside the little terraced house in our motorhome. Luckily the road outside where she was renting was not too busy when we arrived. We took a moment and just looked at where our daughter would be staying for the next year. It looked very sweet on the outside, a lovely little house. It was perfect for students.

One of the other tenants was already there and they had pole position parking, but they very kindly let us know that they had to go food shopping so that we could move into their vacated space. This worked very well and we all started unpacking. This was a whole family procession of backwards and forwards with all the contents from the motorhome to the new house. Once in we dumped everything down and our daughter showed us around. It was perfect inside too; just the right size for three, as she was sharing with two other students, not big but not too small either. It had a lovely little kitchen with a lean-to conservatory that had the freezer, washing machine and other household items in it. It had a nicely decorated downstairs bathroom with bath and shower. It also had a good size lounge, which they could all relax and eat in. All three bedrooms were of a good size. A lovely little garden with a shed, which was set up to be very user friendly for students, no lawnmower but some garden chairs so they could sit out in the summer. Being terraced it felt like they were slightly more protected. All in all a very good find for their student house. We were very impressed.

After we had finished bringing in all the gear and helping with putting the food away and making sure she was happy, it was time for us to say goodbye and good luck. We needed to leave her and let her get on with unpacking and settling in properly. This time it didn't feel so sad, as it had in the first year. It felt more like we were just making sure she was comfortable for the next year. So off we went, back home.

As usual we kept in contact through social media, but she settled in much quicker this year. She had missed university, her friends, the area and the lifestyle, so everything fell into place very quickly.

Don't forget, at the appropriate time, they may have to make a decision about their accommodation for the final year! This might be straight forward if Year Two's accommodation was successful, but they might have to go through the whole process of what they did the previous year if they were not happy with it. There is also some natural shifting about as some of the students may go off to do a year abroad or a year in industry. This may affect some rental groups and they may need to re-think their lodgings. However, by this time they have made more friends and because of this it seems easier for them to organise their third year of accommodation.

This time at Christmas our daughter came home by train. We didn't need to go and collect her so this made it all a lot easier. We would take her back when her university started in January again as she had too much to take with her and we would do the food shopping exercise again, but we were now in a routine, and although it was a big day when we took her back, it was nice to say goodbye to her in a nice little house, with nice housemates in a relaxed environment.

Year Two progressed well.

In Year Two everything seemed to run smoothly. We could call her a fully-fledged university student. Our input was minimal except for collection and dropping off; she no longer required our services as she had in the first year. Even that seemed to have slackened off as she came home more by train this year. All was ticking along well.

16

The graduation year

So Year Three, the final frontier. We had finally made it.

This year is an interesting year, as although your child is in the swing of it as far as knowing exactly what is expected of them, this is a year of pressure. This is the year where they will be expected to achieve what they set out to go to university for.

What we actually found was that Year Three seemed a hard year for both her and us, but for different reasons. For our daughter, I felt she was exhausted in this year. She seemed to be constantly ill and working all hours to achieve her end goal. For me I found that because of her situation I was worrying about her again. I felt that she was ready to come home and I was ready for her to be home. In her mind this was it and she was pursuing it with complete conviction. All that effort and concentration was going into the final hurdle and she wasn't going to let anything or anyone put her off, but this did seem to have a negative effect on her health and how she was coping with the last year.

However on the plus side this wasn't a long year. She

was finished with lectures by the end of April and all of her university work was finished by the end of May, but her rental contract was not finished until the end of June. This was good in one way and bad in another. It gave her some breathing space after the concentrated year to have a bit of time out in a town that she had grown to love. To start to say goodbye to it, the university and her friends and to slowly get her head around coming home and what she would do with the rest of her life. However it was frustrating that the rent still had to be paid when she could have quite easily been home.

Our daughter had made the decision that at this stage a Master's degree was not the way for her to go. She wanted to come back home. She wanted to get out into the work environment and make her own way in society. She felt that she had completed university and now she wanted the next phase to begin.

Talking to her friends, I was quite surprised how undecided some of them were in this year about what they were actually going to do next. Some thought they might have a year out. Some were toying with a Master's. Most seemed to be reluctant to go home, but were not sure what to do. It struck me that they all had a bit of a feel of burnout about them and if they hadn't thought about the end goal earlier they just couldn't get their brains into thinking about what to do next. With us we always said that the university wasn't the end goal, it was a means to an end and pointed directions of possible future avenues to go towards.

So the next thing to organise was her collection. Not a small job. We had to collect her life and bring her back home. Remember I said earlier in the book that they are setting up home when they go to university? Well, when they come back home they want to bring it all back with them. They don't want to get rid of it as they see themselves not being with their parents forever and they will need all of this when they finally leave the nest. So the final collection has to be organised. This is usually done in connection with the final date of rental of the student house. Be aware this is a mammoth task. It is also emotional for them as they are saying goodbye to a part of their lives. Anyway, expect a full day to do final packing, cleaning and collection of the last three years of your child's life. Also expect them to want to spend a bit of time saying goodbye to everything before you leave. As you may have guessed, we brought the motorhome to do this final task and, as you may have guessed, our daughter managed to fill it and then some before we left to go home.

So by the end of June she was home. Life soon settled down and although there was a bit of re-adjusting for everyone it didn't take long for her to be back in our lives. There were differences, subtle differences. She was more grown up, more independent and didn't expect to be waited on anymore. She was a fully functioning adult member of the household. So the university experience to go away and grow up had definitely worked and done its course.

Although back home we hadn't completely severed all ties with university life. We were awaiting her results, which were due in the first week of July, and then we had to go back for the graduation ceremony. You don't have to go back to collect your certificate from the university. You can have it sent to you, but most do go to the graduation ceremony. Having done it now, and in quite spectacular style, I would recommend it.

All the universities carry out the graduation ceremony slightly differently, but there are similarities in them too. Our daughter's university, a big university, had several graduation ceremonies in one day. It was busy, full of colour and excited students. It was a marvellous occasion and as proud parents it is not one to miss. But it is also a full-on day.

Our daughter's graduation took place in mid July, but before this there was plenty of information on the university website. Be careful to just be the invitee to this occasion. It is very important your child should take the lead. It is a big day for them and should be how they want it to be. The extended family need to be sympathetic to this.

As it is a very busy day and full of parents and students, leave plenty of time to get to the university and look into parking as this is a premium on the day. Some universities have agreements with certain park and ride car parks for the graduation weeks. If this is the case you should be able to find out this information on their website. Don't forget you will need to eat. As my daughter's university had beautiful grounds we took a picnic hamper to eat before it all kicked off, as her ceremony was early afternoon. This all worked very well and made it all much more enjoyable. There may be opportunities to eat on the university grounds, but this should be looked at before the day to see what facilities will be available, and to avoid crowds.

For our daughter's graduation there was a full itinerary. Your child will be able to find all this information out and inform you as they see fit. Firstly, they need to find out when and where the ceremony is going to take place and then work backwards from this, and then forwards. By that I mean that once the start time is known you then need to work out when the gown collection for their ceremony is, and once the gown is collected the tickets can then be collected. These will have been ordered previously, and normally this is done by ballot. There is usually a restriction on how many people can go to the actual ceremony; however, most universities show it via a live video link which should take the pressure off if you have extended family who would like to see it.

Guests then need to go to the designated area at the designated time before the ceremony begins. Once all the guests are in the students arrive and fill their designated seats. Our daughter's ceremony lasted about an hour. As her university was a large university the ceremonies were split into faculties. This was then split into different divisions within the same faculty. For example English Language, English Literature, English Literature with Creative Writing and Drama were in the same ceremony.

There were lots of other aspects to the ceremony. There was marketing items such as mugs and pens. Also, graduation souvenirs were available to purchase, such as a souvenir graduation brochure for that year, 'Class of 20XX' T-shirts or 'Leavers 20XX' hoodies, teddy bears, umbrellas etc. She could join an association to become a life-long member of an international network for her university. There were places to have the student's photo taken. There was a professionally recorded graduation DVD which could be pre-ordered if you wanted one. Her university also gave the opportunity to order a graduation stage photo, which showed them crossing the stage and receiving their certificate.

Once the ceremony was over and she had collected her certificate, the faculty photograph took place. I really enjoyed this. The whole faculty was brought together by a very experienced photographer. It took him quite some time to get all the very excited students together and in place so that he could take a picture of them all together with their mortarboard caps on and then with them throwing them into the air. It was an extraordinary sight and one I will not forget in a hurry.

After this had taken place our daughter's university put on a School Celebratory Reception. Again tickets for this had to be ordered previously. The reception was held in a marquee. It included buffet food and drinks. This was a very good cool down for everyone after a very busy day and gave our child time to spend with all her fellow graduates. This was, after all, potentially the last time they were going to see each other.

What a wonderful end to a wonderful journey that began three years earlier. Now onto the final stage of the journey: the home run.

17

The home run

So, the Home Run. What is this about?

Well this is the final piece of the puzzle. This is them finding a job and fitting into the world as a fully functioning member of society. Really, what everyone wants for their children and by no means guaranteed just because they went to University and got a good degree. There are plenty of ex-grads without a job.

So what's the trick? Well there is no trick. Hard graft, strategic manoeuvring and behaving in a way that an employer will want them as an employee are key elements to their success.

Tips? Well, our daughter applied for plenty of work experience placements. She did this in the last semester of her final year, but she started looking for placements in Year Two and went to conferences for the industries she was interested in such as The London Book Fair and Working with Words in this year as well. In total she gained three placements, one of which asked her back for a second time. Obviously when they are looking for placements, they need to think strategically about what they want to end up doing work-wise. They may not know for sure, but they will have an idea as to what industry appeals and what experience would be their goal. Our daughter applied to publishing companies and newspapers. She got placements in two of the largest publishing companies in the UK and one of the largest newspapers in the UK.

She spent a few weeks at the first publishing company and then had a break. None of the placements were consecutive, but in a way this was good as the break in between gave her time to assess her experience with them, update her CV and start seriously looking for a job. Then she had a second placement at the newspaper. She thoroughly enjoyed this experience. They were brilliant and gave her lots of different tasks to do and whilst there she had an article published in the newspaper with her name as the writer. How exciting for a new grad! After this the first publishing company requested her back so she did a further few weeks with them. All the time she was updating her CV and applying for jobs. Then she had the last work experience placement. This was with another large UK publishing company. This company she really enjoyed working for. They were very friendly and once again they gave her lots of different tasks to complete. After her secondment was finished she said goodbye, but before going she spoke to as many key people as she could and gave out her business card to them. This is something she had organised so that when these situations occurred she would be prepared and would come across in a professional manner.

So that was the end of that... or was it? Well, for a

bit it was, and she spent her time ringing agencies and trying to organise interviews. Then she was contacted by the last publishing company and was told there was a job going as a Publishing Assistant in a subsidiary company, was she interested? Oh yes she was! So she sent in her application and waited. Relatively quickly she received a response for an interview. We all held our breath for her. She seemed quite relaxed about it, as she knew where she was going and knew the layout of the company. We waited… and then she was contacted for a second interview. Again, we waited. The next thing I knew I heard her on the phone and there were squeals of delight coming from her room. I knew from experience that I had to be patient and wait until she was ready to tell me what was going on. This time, however, I did not have to wait long. She burst into our office and through tears and laughter told me that she had got the job! Oh my God, how awesome was that? And how proud did I feel at that moment? VERY! It is, after all, what you are hoping will happen for them. It is the winning goal of a long and extraordinary journey. The best outcome you can hope for. She obviously had to wait for a confirmation email and then a letter. Everything was in order and looked perfect. She started on 7th December 2015. So this all happened quite quickly bearing in mind she didn't get her degree results until July 7th and graduated on July 22nd. By the beginning of December she had her first proper full-time job working for a serious publishing company. I think this was job well done, and congratulations to her.

On December 7th 2015 she did her first day and to

date she is still with this company and is very happy in her new role. She is PA to the Publishing Director and carries out all related duties.

After starting at the publishing company she was contacted by her university. They had seen on LinkedIn that she had got a job with a publishing company, and they asked her to go back to the university to speak to the students to tell them what opportunities were out there for English students. This time she was going back as a speaker to give advice!

This was amazing to me. My little girl who used to be shy and timid was going back to her university to stand in a lecture hall full of students and give them tips and advice about what was out there for them. This showed how much she had grown whilst away and what a good university education in the fullest sense can do for them, with a little good guidance from home.

I hope you have enjoyed our journey and that this experience has been of some help to you for when your journey begins.